How to Imp SAP HCM for ICT Corporation – Time Attendence And Payroll Processes

DAVID JONES

DAVID JONES

The book will teach HR professionals how to use SAP HCM for compensation management by mapping key business processes to the TIME AND ATTENDANCE PAYROLL Process functionality in SAP HCM. It explains how SAP provides a robust framework for implementing processes, and teaches how to integrate compensation management techniques with other HR processes.

CONTENTS

B. PAYROLL PROCESS

ACKNOWLEDGMENTS

I would like to express my gratitude to the many people who saw me through this book; to all those who provided support, talked things over, read, wrote, offered comments, allowed me to quote their remarks and assisted in the editing, proofreading and design.

I would like to thank SAP Japan for enabling me to publish this book. Above all I want to thank my wife and the rest of my family, who supported and encouraged me in spite of all the time it took me away from them. It was a long and difficult journey for them.

I would like to thank Yamamoto, Bobby, Gamal Kounafa and Alexander Dalke for helping me in the process of selection and editing.

Last and not least: I beg forgiveness of all those who have been with me over the course of the years and whose names I have failed to mention.

A. TIME AND ATTENDANCE

This chapter provides a framework for the Leave Request and Overtime and Allowance business processes identified in ICTROI. The objective is to:

- ✓ Assist with understanding scenarios within the business process
- ✓ Support the business and consultants during the realization phase

The Leave Request and Overtime and Allowances processes have been grouped under heading HR-100-Time and Attendance Business Process due to their relation to the Time and Attendance module in SAP. This document will describe these processes as separate scenarios. The following scenarios will be covered in this document:

- ✓ *Leave Requests*
- ✓ *Overtime and Allowances*

I. LEAVE REQUEST

1. Overview of the Scenario

Leave is defined as any absence from work. Each type of absence is set up as a leave code. These leave codes then map to absence types. All Leave is processed through Infotype 2001 (Absences). There are two types of absence, those that reduce a balance (Absence Quotas – Infotype 2006 eg. Annual Leave), and those that do not. Once an employees' quota type is exhausted an error message will appear stating they do not have enough entitlement for that period of leave.

Employees apply for leave by using the Leave Request Form in Employee Self Service (ESS).The Leave request form will workflow to the employees' Manager for approval, then depending on which type of leave the employee is requesting the absence will be updated in SAP, workflow for further approval, or workflow to the Payroll area for processing. Refer to 2.1.3.1 Absence Type and Workflow Approval.

Entry of Absence:

- ✓ Type of Leave
- ✓ Date from
- ✓ Date to
- ✓ Hours (if less and normal standard day)
- ✓ Note for Approver – free text field

If it is a full-day absence, once the user has entered the absence type, absence dates and press the "Review" button, the system will automatically populate the Duration hour's field using the employees daily work hours from Infotype 0007. If the absence is for part of the day, the user will also need to enter the hours absent. When the employee submits the leave request for approval and once fully approved, the absence details are saved in Infotype 2001 (Absences) and the employee is notified.

Leave Type Requiring Documentary Evidence

Certain leave types require the employee to provide supporting documentation to the manager prior to approval. Refer to 2.1.3.1 Absence Type and Workflow Approval. When the manager approves the leave a checkbox appears for the manager to check indicating the documentation has been sighted.

Leave approval workflow

The leave request workflow is triggered when an employee submits a leave request in ESS. The leave request is sent as a work item to the employee's manager (or delegated leave approver) for approval. The manager will receive a notification in their Outlook Inbox advising of the leave request. The manager can click on the link to go to the UWL Inbox to process the work item. When the manager executes the work item, the leave request is displayed to the manager with all the details of the leave request such as:

- ✓ Employee name
- ✓ Leave Type
- ✓ Dates leave requested for
- ✓ Notes entered by the employee

If the leave request is approved, the system creates a record in Infotype 2001 for the employee. The system sends a notification to the employee advising them of the leave approval. If an approver rejects the leave request, the system will not create a record in Infotype 2001. Instead, the request is sent as a work item to the ESS inbox of the employee. When the employee executes the work item, the leave request is displayed along with any notes that the manager may have added for rejection. The employee can decide to change the request and resubmit it or withdraw the request. If the request is resubmitted, it is sent to the manager again for approval and follows the process described above. If the request is withdrawn, the workflow is terminated. Employee Self Service also provides an employee with an overview and the current status of all leave requests they have submitted in a given period of time. Only leave which has been applied through ESS is displayed in the leave request overview.

When required, employees can use the Overview of Leave

option to:

- ✓ Cancel a leave request which has not yet been approved. If the leave request has not been approved, cancellation of the request does not require approval. The workflow for the leave request is automatically deleted.
- ✓ Cancel a leave request which has been approved. The cancellation of an approved leave request also requires approval. The cancellation request is forwarded to the employee's manager or selected approver via workflow. Upon approval of the cancellation, the leave request is deleted from Infotype 2001.
- ✓ Withdraw a cancellation request that has not yet been approved or processed. A cancellation that has been processed/approved cannot be withdrawn. In such cases, the employee must submit a new leave request for approval.

The overview of existing leave entitlement described below is based on the standard ESS service. A number of leave types such as Annual Leave, Sick Leave, and Long Service Leave require a balance to be maintained. These balances are held against Absence Quota Types for each leave type. Within SAP, the Time Evaluation program (RPTIME00 driver) is run on a monthly basis to calculate the allocations of leave accrual and / or entitlements against Absence Quotas. The Absence Quota Infotype is used to store an employee's leave entitlement (not accrual information).

The Time Evaluation program updates the absence quotas records when the following has occurred:

- ✓ A leave anniversary date is reached (as per the date type from Date Specifications Infotype – 0041). The anniversary date is the date in which the leave accrual becomes an entitlement. For example long service leave will accrue but will only transfer to an entitlement after a NSW employee has had 10 years continuous service. Long service leave entitlement may be different between Australian states and territories, and New Zealand.

✓ Leave request has been approved (which reduces entitlement)
✓ A quota correction is made for entitlement.
✓ Annual leave is accrued on a monthly basis
✓ Sick leave is accrued on each employee's anniversary date

Employees are able to display an overview of their leave entitlement as at the current date in ESS. The data is derived from the employee's Infotype 2006 record which does not include accrual details and is subject to when Time Evaluation was last ran within R/3. The accrual portion of the leave cannot be used unless it has rolled over to entitlement. The following describes the fields and functions which employees are able to view:

✓ Time Account: Leave balance type eg. Annual Leave
✓ Deductible to: Deduction period (the period in which the employee can deduct the quota eg. up to 31.12.9999)
✓ Entitlement: (specifies an employee's total entitlement for a particular period – excluding accrual details)
✓ Leave Deduction: Used (specifies the portion of the leave entitlement which has been taken)
✓ Leave Balance: Available balance (displays the remaining balance for the entitlement, ie this is what

the employee still has available to use). Accrued leave cannot be taken until it has rolled over to entitlement.

2. Master Data and Organizational Data

No	Master Data Requirements
1	Personnel number
2	Username
3	Organizational assignment - current holder of a valid position
4	Structural approval rights, (ie the Line Manager will be in a chief position of an org unit, and the 2nd line manager will be in the next structural level above.)
5	Custom Organization Management Relationships
6	Type of leave
7	Date from
8	Date to
9	Duration
10	Note for approver

Absence Types and Workflow Approval

The business process flows for leave requests varies slightly for each leave type. Business process flows diagrams have been created for this document by grouping leave types with similar approval paths and supporting documentation requirements. Approval paths and supporting documentation requirements are listed in the following table. Absence Types and Workflow Approval, these are grouped intro 4 Process

flow diagrams.

Absence		Approval Matrix							
Type	Description	Mgr 1	Mgr 2	EGM	HRBL	HRC	HR EGM	PAY ROLL	Doc
ACC1	ACC 1st Week	X			X	X		X	
ACC2	ACC 2nd Week onwards	X			X	X		X	
ADOP	Adoption Leave	X	X		X			X	X
AL	Annual Leave	X							
AWAY	Away Leave	X				X			
BRVE	Compassionate/Bereavement	X							
CARP	Carer's Leave (Paid)	X							
CARW	Carer's Leave (W/O Pay)	X							
CONT	Contractor Leave	X							
CSL	Community Service Leave	X							
DEFP	Defence Leave	X						X	X
DOIL	Day off in Lieu	X							
FTEA	Fixed Term emp absence	X							
JURY	Jury Service	X						X	X
LSL	Long Service Leave	X	X						
LSL1	Long Service Leave <4wks	X							
LSL2	Long Service Leave>4wks	X	X						
LWOU	Leave w/o pay unauthorised	X							
LWP1	Leave without pay < 3 wks	X							
LWP2	Leave without pay > 3wks	X	X	X	X	X	X		
MATL	Maternity Leave	X			X	X		X	X
PATL	Paternity Leave	X			X	X		X	X
PATP	Paternity Leave Paid	X			X	X		X	X
PICN	Picnic Day	X							
PLWP	Personal /Sick Leave	X							

	Paid								
PWOP	Personal /Sick Leave Unpaid	X							
REG	Regional Holiday	X							
RELO	Relocation Leave	X							
SCB	Salary Cont. Benefit								
SHOW	Show Day	X							
SLUP	Sick leave (unpaid)	X							
SLWP	Sick leave (paid)	X							
SPEC	Special Leave	X							
STDY	Study Leave	X							
WCPO	Workers Comp Pos 45 wks	X			X	X		X	
WCPR	Workers Comp Pre 45 wks	X			X	X		X	

3. Process flow diagram

a. Leave types requiring Manager only approval

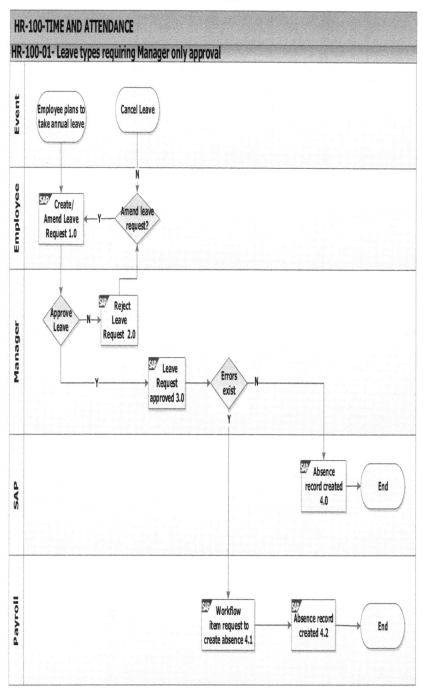

b. Apply for Adoption / Maternity/ Paternity Leave

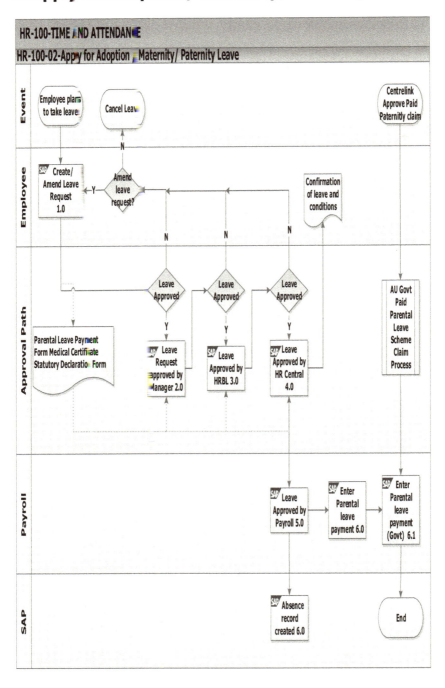

c. Apply for Leave requiring Manager and EGM only

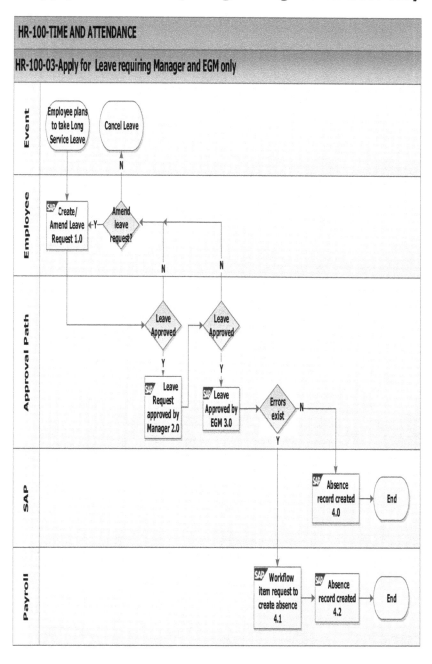

d. Apply for Defense Force Leave / Jury Service

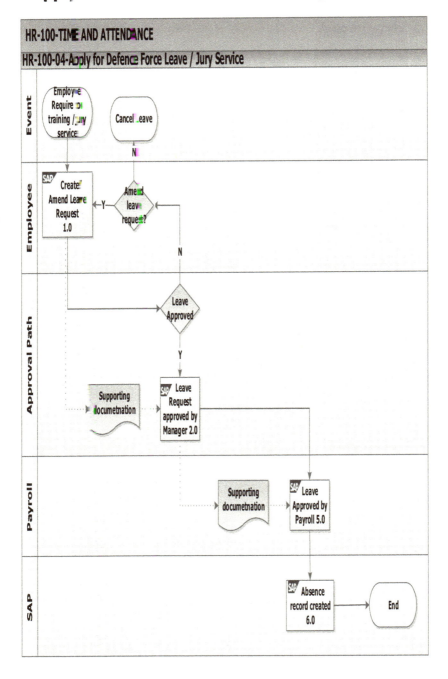

4. Scenario Overview Tab

NO	Process step	Business condition	Security role	Expected results
1	Employee creates leave request in ESS	Employee is entitled to take leave under conditions of employment. Leave quota (if applicable is available)	Employee	Leave request is workflowed to Line Mananger. Email notfication is sent to mananger. Absence is created in InfoType 2001 (Absences) as a locked record.
2	Manager rejects leave	Sufficient leave quota available Documentation not provided Business requirements do not permit absence during requested period.	Manager	Leave request is workflowed back to employee. Employee may amend leave request as appropriate.
3	Manager approves leave	Employee has suffcient quota availablefor quota based leave. Documentation is sighted if requred. Sufficient resources are available to deliver business requirements	Manager	Absence record is unlocked Absence quota is updated and entitlement is reduced for quota based leave. Email notification is sent to employee.
4	Absence record updated in SAP. (If there are no errors)			Absence record is saved against InfoType 2001. Absence quota is updated and entitlement is reduced for quota based leave.

5. Interfaces

List and provide an overview of any reports that will be required or generated from this scenario.

Transaction	Report Name	Frequency	Usage
ZHR3_LV_R_06	Annual Leave Projection		
ZHR3_LV_R_06_MGR	Annual Leave Projection		
ZHR3_LV_R_02	Employee Leave History		
ZHR3_LV_R_02_MGR	Employee Leave History		
ZHR3_HR_R_31	Leave & Timesheet Compliance Report		
ZHR_LV_R_03	HR Long Leave Accrual Report		
ZHR_LV_R_04	NZ Leave Report		
ZHR_LV_R_04_MGR	NZ Leave Report		
ZHR_LV_R_07	Long Service Leave Projection		
ZHR_LV_R_07_MGR	Long Service Leave Projection		
ZHR_LV_R_08	Display Leave Requests (Database)		
ZHR_LV_R_09	Delete Leave Requests (Database)		
ZHR3_LV_R_01	Employee Leave Balance		
ZHR3_LV_R_01_MGR	Employee Leave Balance		
BW Report	Leave Combi Report		
BW Report	Leave History by Employee Report		
BW Report	Leave Projection by Employee Report		

6. Workflow

List and provide an overview of any workflow that will be required or generated from this scenario.

Workflow Id	Workflow Name	Description	Object/ Class
WS91000009	ZLVERQST	Leave Request	BUS7007
WS91000006	ZFAL_ABSCANC	Cancel Leave Request	BUS7007

II. OVERTIME AND ALLOWANCES

1. Overview of the Scenario

This process is used to create an overtime payment. ICTROI will pay Overtime/standby payments to employees as required by the appropriate Awards and under particular circumstances. In general, exempt employees are not eligible for overtime/standby payments. All overtime will require the approval from an employee's 1st Level Manager prior to completing overtime work.

Claims for overtime and allowances paid on a per-claim basis can be made online via ESS in the SAP Portal. Only employees eligible to submit a request will be able to enter the respective time or kilometres allowance request forms. Shift allowance is not entered via the Overtime and Allowances form.

Claims are workflowed to the business unit manager or WBS manager if different. A background job is run in SAP to upload overtime and allowance claims entered in ESS. The Payroll area will run reports prior to the pay run to identify and correct anomalies. If a claim is rejected the employee will be required to resubmit the claim.

Where eligible employees are not able to enter overtime or allowance claims via the SAP Portal they will be required to manually enter the hours they worked using an excel spreadsheet. The spreadsheet will be forwarded to the 1st Level Manager for approval. Once the claim has been approved, the Manager will forward the overtime/standby spreadsheet to payroll for processing. In this situation transaction (PA71) is used to enter data for a group or more than one employee at a time.

The following allowances can be claimed be employees via Employee Self Service

- ✓ Overtime Allowance
- ✓ On Call Allowance
- ✓ Cal out Allowance
- ✓ Kilometre Allowance

Employees are only able to enter claims requests for allowances they are entitled to under their employment conditions. (Based on the Additional Time Id field in Infotype 0007).

Shift allowance is paid as a recurring payment and by Time Evaluation for employees that are entitled under their employment conditions (Based on the Award Category Id field in Infotype 0016).

2. Master Data and Organizational Data

No	Master Data Requirements
1	Personnel number
2	Username
3	Organizational assignment - current holder of a valid position
4	Structural approval rights, (ie the Line Manager will be in a chief position of an org unit, and the 2nd line manager will be in the next structural level above.)
5	Custom Organization Management Relationships
6	Claim Date
7	Start and End timesare validated to ensure no conflict with other entries or your Normal working hours.
8	Type (e.g. overtime, on-call or call-back) isselected from the Dropdown list.
9	Call Nois optional.
10	Customer iss optional, only a valid Customer code can be selected.
11	Cost Centre is only entered if it differs from the user's Cost Centre, click on Select to display a listing of all valid Cost Centres
12	WBS code can de entered if the claim relates to a Project, this field is optional.
13	Reason

3. Process Flow Diagram

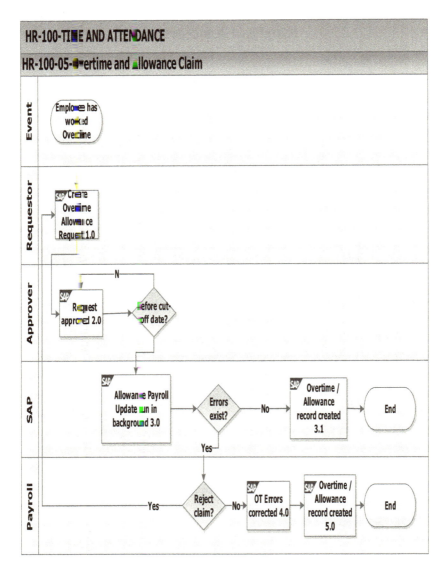

4. Scenario Overview Table

No	Process step	Business condition	Security role	Expected results
1	Claim for overtime or allowance is created in ESS by employee or manager on behalf of employee	The overtime hours have already been worked.	1st Level Manager Employee	Overtime or allowance request is created and workflowed for approval. Email notification is sent to approver. The approver will recieve a workflow item to approve
2	Claim for overtime or allowance is approved in ESS by Manager, WBS Manager or 2nd Level Manager	If the claim was submitted by the employee, the claim will workflow to the employes line manager. If the overtime was worked for a different WBS the claim will workflow to the WBS approver. If the claim was submited by the manager on behalf of the employee the claim will workfolw to the 2nd level mananger.	1st Level Manager WBS Manager 2nd Level Manager	Overtime or allowance request approved. Save claim in InfoType 2010
3	Allowance Payroll Update program is run in the background to update overtime and allowance records in payroll	Approved Overtime Allowance Request is before Payroll cut-off date (7th of each month)		Overtime and allowance records are created in payroll
4	Run overtime and allowance reports to identify errors	Report run daily between the 20th and the 8th of the next month prior to payroll close off to ensure errors are identified and corrected.		Errors are identified or claim rejected. Employee may need to reapply.
5	Overtime and allowance entries amended			Overtime or allowance entries amended

5. Interfaces

List and provide an overview of any interfaces that will be required or generated from this scenario.

Transaction	Interface Name	In/Out	File Format
ZPY_P_OT_ALLOW_UPD	Allowance Payroll Update		

6. Reports

List and provide an overview of any reports that will be required or generated from this scenario.

Transaction	Report Name	Frequency	Usage
ZHR_OT_R_01	Category Verification Report		
ZHR_OT_R_02	OT & Allowance Request Report	Once a month	Report of overtime and allowances claimed for the month.
ZHR_OT_R_03	Allowances claimed during 12 months		
ZHR_OT_R_04	Allowances manually paid report		
ZHR_OT_R_05	Hours and kilometres paid report		
ZPY_R_OT_ERROR	Allowance Payroll Update Error Report	Daily between 20th and 8th of the month	Used to identify errors
BW Report	OT and Allowances Report		

7. Enhancements

List and provide an overview of any enhancement that will be required or generated from this scenario.

Program Name	Description	Transaction Code
SAPLZOT	Overtime and Allowance Maintenance	ZHR_T_OT_ALLOW
SAPLZOT_ALLOW	Overtime and allowance Category Maintenance	ZHR_T_OT_CAT
SAPLZOT_ALLOW	Allowance Pay Area Lock	ZPY_T_OT_RUN

B. PAYROLL PROCESS

The payroll is run at a specific point in time, to calculate an employee's basic remuneration, special payments, overtime payments or bonuses. This document provides a framework for the Payroll Processing business process identified in ICTROI. The objective is to:

- ✓ Assist with understanding scenarios within the business process
- ✓ Support the business and consultants during the realization phase

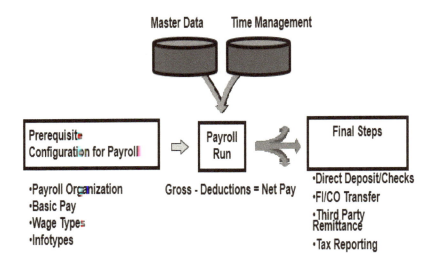

The Payroll Processing business process is the culmination of HR master data changes and transactional data input as a result of other HR Business Processes. These business processes include:

- ✓ **Recruitment Request – New Hire Business Process**
- ✓ **Personnel Change Request Business Process Document**
- ✓ **Time and Attendance -Overtime and Allowance Processing**
- ✓ **Time and Attendance - Leave Request**
- ✓ **Merit Review**
- ✓ **Incentives and ITA**
- ✓ **Termination Process**

1. Overview of the Scenario

This scenario documents the monthly Payroll process used to process payroll for ICTROI employees. Prior to processing the pay run, the Payroll Business Unit is responsible for ensuring all regular data maintenance is performed during the payroll period. This includes data maintenance on the following:

- ✓ New Starters
- ✓ Terminations
- ✓ Payment maintenance
- ✓ Deduction maintenance
- ✓ Superannuation contribution maintenance
- ✓ Tax data maintenance
- ✓ Other data maintenance
- ✓ Bonus and Commissions
- ✓ Leave
- ✓ Overtime and Allowances

ICTROI pays all permanent and fixed term employees on a monthly basis. Employees' salary is deposited into the banking system on the eighteenth of each month, or the first working day before. Payment is made up of approximately two weeks in arrears and two weeks in advance. Payment is made up of one full month, i.e. payment for 01.01.2016 – 31.01.2016 is received on the 16th of January. Casual employees are paid on a weekly basis. New starters who commence after the 9th day of the month will be paid in the following month. Payslips are available on ESS (Employee Self Service) on the 18th of the month. Preparation for processing for the pay run begins on the 8th of the month, to allow for payroll to be simulated and error logs checked and all errors rectified prior the final pay run.

2. Master Data and Organizational Data

No	Master Data Requirements
1	Employee id
2	Organisation assignment
3	Work schedule
4	Planned work times
5	Basic pay
6	Transactional data and from other HR business processes

3. Process Flow Diagram

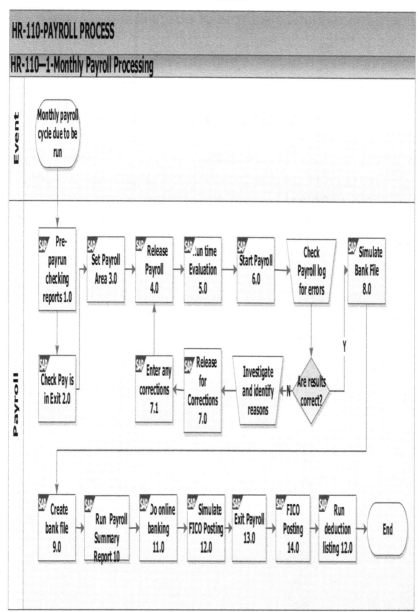

4. Scenario Overview Table

You can simulate payroll for individual employees before doing the regular payroll run for all the employees. In this manner, you recognize sources of errors in time to make corrections before the regular payroll run. A simulation run corresponds to a regular payroll run with the following restrictions:

- ✓ The results of a simulated payroll run are not saved in the database.
- ✓ You can view and print the results in the payroll log.
- ✓ The current payroll period in the payroll control record is not changed.
- ✓ The steps Release payroll and Exit payroll do not apply.

	Process step	Business condition	Security role	Expected results
1	Run Payrun checking reports	Begin payroll checking reports on the 8th of the month	Payroll Maintenance	All reports run, any errors identified and corrected.
2	Check pay in is exit		Payroll Adminstrator	Payroll status is at **Exit Payroll** as indicated by the green tick
3	Set payroll area		Payroll Adminstrator	Payroll area set to correct area
4	Release Payroll		Payroll Adminstrator	Payroll status is at **Released Correction** as indicated by the green tick
5	Run time evaluation		Payroll Adminstrator	Time evaluation Run, error log displayed.
6	Start Payroll		Payroll Adminstrator	Pay run, error log displayed.
7.0	Release for corrections	Repeat steps 5-7 until all errors have been corrected and logs are error free	Payroll Adminstrator	
7.1	Enter any corrections			Errors corrected
8	Simulate and create Banking file (Run in TEST)		Payroll Adminstrator	File is created, Errors displayed
8.1	Simulate and create Banking file	Errors identified in TEST mode identified and corrected prior to running	Payroll Adminstrator	File is created. Program id run date noted.
9	Create bank file		Payroll Adminstrator	Bank file is downloaded
10	Run Payroll Summary Report		Payroll Adminstrator	Report run. Total pay amounts
11	Banking		Payroll Adminstrator	Bank file uploaded
12	Simulate FICO		Payroll Adminstrator	Posting document simulated
13	Exit Payroll	All errors corrected	Payroll Adminstrator	Payroll is in exit mode
14	Post FICO	Payroll is in exit	Payroll Adminstrator	Posting document created
15	Run Deduction Listing and email		Payroll Adminstrator	Report downloaded for each deduction type.

5. Interfaces

List and provide an overview of any interfaces that will be required or generated from this scenario.

Transaction	Interface Name	In/Out	File Format
ZHR_PY_I_01	Upload Data into table T5QSC		
ZHR_PY_I_02	Superannuation Fund Upload		
ZHR3_PY_INCR	Upload Annual Pay Increases		

6. Reports

List and provide an overview of any reports that will be required or generated from this scenario.

Transaction	Report Name/Variant	Frequency	Usage
PC00_M99_CWTR	AU_MANUAL_PAY (Manual Pay Report)	Per Payrun,	Used to check all Manual Pay entries against List Pay folder to ensure all employees paid via Westpac Corporate Online have had a Manual Pay (WT3351) entered in IT0015.
PC00_M99_CWTR	AU_TERM_PAY (Terminated Employees)	Per Payrun - after Terminations and Commission s have been entered.	Used to check that all terminated employees receiving a payment are correct. Payments listed are usually for Commission, Overtime or for employees that have terminated later in the month. The report will also pick up Re-Hire actions run by HR but not by Payroll. These must be checked with HR before payment.
PC00_M99_CWTR	AU_COMPARISON (Variance Report)	Per Payrun – After 2nd run	This report will display net pay for this pay and last pay. Used to check employee records where there are large differences. Differences will usually be a result of Commissions or Overtime/SBAL.
PC00_M99_CWTR	AU_BANK_TFR (Net Over 10K Report)	Per Payrun – after changes from Mat/Pat/LW OP report	Used to check the 30 highest and lowest paid employees. Used to find errors with SBAL or OT.
S_PHO_48000510	PAYRUN_LWOP (Mat Pat LWOP Report)	Per Payrun	Used to report on all employees on Maternity, Paternity, LWOP>3wks and Unauthorised LWOP in the specified period
S_PHO_48000510	PAYRUN_AU_SALSAC (LWOP WITH SALARY SACRIFICE SUPER)	Per Payrun	Used to report on any employees who have had LWOP and also a salary sacrifice component
S_PHO_48000510	PAYRUN_SSCOMP (SALARY SACRIFICE SUPER COMPARISON)	Per Payrun	Used to report on any employees with both a IT0008 and IT 0220 record. Check for any differences.
S_PHO_48000510	PAYRUN_AU_IT08	Per Payrun	Used to report on any employees with IT0008
S_PHO_48000510	PAYRUN_AU_IT220	Per Payrun	Used to report on any employees with IT 0220
S_PHO_48000510	PAYRUN_AU_TAX (TAX IT188 CHECK)	Per Payrun	Used to report on any employees with any changes made in IT0188
S_PHO_48000510	PAYRUN_TRP (TRP CHECKING)	Per Payrun	Used to report on any employees with any changes made in IT0008
S_PHO_48000510	BASIC_PAY_AU (TRP Checking)	Per Payrun	Used to report on any employees with any changes made in IT0008 including the user who made the changes. This will also identify new starters, locked and unlocked

Transaction	Report Name/Variant	Frequency	Usage
S_PHO_480005 0	OT_INPUT (Overtime Report)	Per Payrun	Used to report on any employees with any changes made in IT2010 including the user who made the changes. Amounts used for checking.
S_PHO_480005 D	AU_Reffeal	Per Payrun	Run after payclose and sent to Recruitment.
PC00_M13_ATOR_PS	ATO Report	Per month	Used to upload tax file numbers to ATO website.
PC00_M99_CWTR	Deductions Listing report	After payrun	Used to download deduction amounts. Deduction listing sent corresponding party.
ZHR3_SUPER	Superannuation report for upload to Russell	Per month	Used to update super files and uploaded onto the Russell super website.
ZHR_PY_R_03	Payment summary download	Annually or as required	Used to view and download Payment summaries required annually or as requested by employees.
ZHR_PY_R_01	ABS Report (Australian Bureau of Statistics report	Annual	Legislative requirement
ZHR_PY_R_02	Custom Wage Type Reporter		
ZHR_PY_R_04	Payment Summary Report		
ZHR_PY_R_05	Cost Centre Report		
ZHR_PY_R_06	Employee Summary Report		
ZHR3_SUPER_EXITS	Superannuation Reporting – Exits		
ZHR3_SUPER_EXITS_OLD	Superannuation Interface for Exits		
ZHR3_SUPER_NEW_MEMB	Superannuation Reporting – New Members		
ZHR3_SUPER_NEWMEMB_O	Superannuation Interface for New Members		
ZHR3_SUPER_OLD	Superannuation Interface Program		
ZHR3_SUPER_UPDATE	Superannuation Reporting – Updates		
ZHR3_SUPER_UPDATE_O	Superannuation Interface Program		
ZHR3_SHOW_TRP_AS_DF	Show TRP statement in PDF format		

7. Forms

List and provide an overview of any forms that will be required or generated from this scenario.

Form Name	Description	Transaction Code	Output (Print/Email./Fax/EDI)
Payslip	Payment advice	PC00_M13_CALC (remittance advice)	PDF viewed in ESS
Payment Summary	Summary of year to date used for taxation purposes	ZHR_PY_R_03	PDF viewed in ESS, can also be emailed
TRP Statement	TRP Statement	ZHR3_SHOW_TRP_AS_PDF	PDF viewed in ESS

ABOUT THE AUTHOR

Innovative and Disruptive Technology Thought Leader with more than 18 years of successful track record of delivering and executing global and complex business transformation initiatives for multiple global clients with special focus in High Tech and Manufacturing Industry sectors. Continue to serve Global, Fortune 500, and mid size firms in various capacities such as Delivery Leader, Delivery Quality Assurance, and Solution Architect. Focused on Innovative Technology and Business Operations, Business Re-engineering and Large Scale System Deployments. Delivering innovative customer solutions focused around Customer Experience, Cloud & SaaS, Call Center, eCommerce (B2B & B2C), Mobility, & Product Management.

High tech (Software & Semiconductor Manufacturing) Subject Matter Specialist recognized for successfully delivering cutting edge best practice based solutions to premier High tech clients. In-depth and hands on understanding of entire 'Lead to Cash' business process in SAP Cloud for Customer (C4C), hybris eCommerce, SAP ECC, and SAP CRM.

Specific focus areas include Cloud deployment integration options (Hybrid Vs Standalone), Configure, Price and Quote (CPQ), Product Configuration (Make to Order & Engineering to Order), Revenue Recognition etc.

Domain Expertise: hybris eCommerce, SAP C4C - Cloud for Customer. SAP ECC 6.0 - Sales and Distribution (SD) including Pricing, Sales & Service contracts, Payment card processing, Rev Rec, Variant Configurator, Manufacturing, 3PL, Logistics, and Billing. SAP E-Commerce (B2B & B2C), IPC, SAP CRM 7.0 - Sales, Service, and Marketing